... IN
SEARCH OF
REDEMPTION
THE JOURNEY OF A LIFETIME

By
Andrew Smith

. . . In Search of Redemption The Journey of a Lifetime
© 2024 Andrew Smith

Kipekee Press
Hamilton, ON, Canada
Kipekeepress.com
info@kipekeepress.com

ISBN: 978-1-990728-38-9 paperback
ISBN: 978-1-990728-39-6 hardcover
ISBN: 978-1-990728-40-2 ebook

Also by the Author

Rebuilding Janise: A Family's First Year After A Stroke
. . . a life in motion (in movement through time)

Dedication

to She who is...
caregiver & teacher
the first one

the first one
to nurture & provide
for me

for me
to be
who i am today

today i am me
because
she is she

to She who is...
a moral example
always giving

giving her all
asking nothing
in return

i try to return
all she gave
to this world

my world is this way
as she taught
me well

to She who is...
many things
holds many titles

these titles collected
over the span
of her years

daughter & sister
auntie &
grandmother

as she is my mother
my foundation
in a word she is LOVE

Table of Contents

Foreword

This our only option
There is but one way
The direction we must take
No other alternative exists but...

Forward intime

And our actions
Will impact and change
Our existence and destiny
As we move through our world step-by-step

Forward intime

Though solutions are at a distance
And at times we feel stalled
Surrendering hope in the present
Yet hold faith in our future - so we continue

Forward intime

And slowly we will see
From good seeds
Come good trees with succulent fruits
The results of our labour as we toil

Forward intime

Our focus now switched
From what was, to what is
The possibilities available
And what could truly be by moving

Forward intime

We will however live each day
Enjoy the imperfect journey
The freshly paved roads and the potholes
The dirt roads and rough gravel on the way

Forward intime

Prelude

Not the story
But they help me through it
Relive it
& experience it

Not the memory
But they help me recall it
recount it
& Be in it

Not the comfort
But they ease me through it
Soothe it
& confront it

Not a weakness
As they make me fearless
Powerful
& resilient

As the pools of my eyes
Fill up
& capacity is reached
I will let go

Unstoppable my tears will flow
Matching my stream of consciousness
Freeing me
& cleansing my soul

My tears
Not the story
But they help me
Deal with it

Chapter 1

The Awakening

i.
Alarmed

awakened from your slumber
you are alert
and concerned
yet unaware of time

the time now
the time past
and all that time
in-between

it is three-thirty
in the morning
you are alarmed
and i would be to

the usual rapid-fire questions
asking about our sons
where they are
and how they are

this time your focus
is our daughter, though

born after our first son
born before our second son

yes born
into this cruel world
but cruelly born still
still born

you are now at that time
decades ago
you are alarmed
and i would be to

you ask "where is she"
i answer sleeping in her room
my voice strong and assuring
committed to this lie

reassured by my words
and taking comfort in my deception
you return to your slumber
i watch you peacefully fall asleep

it is four-thirty
in the morning
i am wide awake
but you are no longer

alarmed

ii.
…and I arise

before the sun
in the dark quiet
of the morning

with a soul content
mind and body rested
alert and aware
ready

…and i arise
full
filled with potential
open to possibilities
to BE

to meet that which greets me
to see my way
above
around
and through this day

...and i arise
yes, before the sun
but redefined
redeemed
shedding the day before
yesterday

now reenergized
and enthusiastic
inspired and motivated
and always
leading with LOVE

...and i arise

iii.
Dreamland

Eyes now open.
It is the first sign of the transition.
Alert, aware and well rested from your travels.
Now in this space, this place.
Coming from the land of dreams.

Where all is possible.
Where there are no restrictions.
And you are free of rules, laws, and preconceptions.
Limitless.
Able to explore the depths of your imagination.

Now in this place, this space.
You struggle with retention.
Your memory of all of the scenarios lived.
The actions taken and the lessons learned.
The full scope of all that took place, in your nightly journey.

Now in this space, this place.
This physical world.
Where you do spend most of your time.
But your connection is lost to the purpose.
The practical application of your learnings from the nightly journey.

It is through sleep.
This nightly regimen.
You rest and recover.
You also process your life.
And have the potential to progress your life.

Now in this space, this place.
Dream's messages are encrypted.
An unfinished puzzle.
With the depth of great knowledge.
To be unleashed once solved.

iv.
It's Good to Be Here

And it is good
To be here

There was a time
When it was not

That time created
The me you see

When I was lost
With no direction

Unguided and unfocused
Out of control

And it is good
To be here

Having made it
To the other side

Armed with lessons
Of the journey

Out from the path
Of the storm

Now healing wounds
That resurface

Still I am waiting
For the pain to end

And it is good
To be here

I could have been
Anywhere else

It could have ended
Some other way

There could have been
No future days

And it is good
To be here

As it is here
Where I be

Like the needle
That fits the groove

Like the song
That fits the mood

And it is good
To be here

I do agree
This place is for me

I have found comfort
A safe space

My absence will never
Be too long

As it is here
Where I belong

And it is good
To be here

V.
I Am Here

On arrival
I was under construction
In the process of building
Changing and growing

On arrival
I was content
In quiet reflection
Strong and independent

On arrival
I was seeking and searching
I was alone
In denial of my loneliness

And then
I found you and you found me
Together we found even more
Our purpose and our future

And then
I embraced your disruption

The whirlwind that came along
Your beautiful unsettling noise

At that moment
I found someone to change for
To grow and build with
To protect and hunt for

At that moment
I found someone to be open with
To hold and be held by
To share all my love with

And then
You fell down
All the way down
With no promise of a future

But I was there
Right by your side
To pick you up
I picked you up and held you close

But I was there
Filled with hope
My faith stayed strong
Since that moment
That I found you

And I am here
To keep you up

And I am here
To build you up

And I am here
To love you up

For life
And for our lives

This holds true
As I believe in you

vi.
Human

A sinner and a saint
A lover and a fighter
A winner and a loser
A taker and a provider

I am simply human
What about you?

I mostly do the right thing
But sometimes I don't
I often wish you the best
But sometimes I won't

I will love my enemies
I take the high road
But would really feel better
If I dropped down to their level

Your analysis is correct
Your judgement is sound
I stand before you guilty
And now convicted as charged

A sinner and a saint
A lover and a fighter
A winner and a loser
A taker and a provider

I am simply human
So now, what about you?

vii.
Humanity

I have no need to prove it.
You must remove your preconceptions,
And use the eyes God gave you.
The windows to your soul.

As they will reveal,
The truth you already knew.
There's no fraction before you,
Nothing short of the whole.

Deserving of all,
This life has to give.
With the freedom to explore,
The life that I live.

I stand on the outside,
Of your court of judgement.
It holds nothing no authority,
Over my mind or my soul.

I have no need to prove it.
You must remove your preconceptions,

And use the eyes God gave you.
The windows to your soul.

So do as I've asked,
Or do nothing at all.
As you have freedom of choice
To express your own voice.

viii.
I Can

it is clear to me
revealed for my eyes to see
not locked away i have the key
or hidden and shrouded in mystery

but i can't

it is truly my reality
this circumstance not dismal to me
this journey is my destiny
i travel it's path with autonomy

but i can't

long and winding is the way
filled with challenges are my days
the gains occur though they are few
i won't allow this to cloud my view

but i can't

can't give up or let it go
can't drop or fall from every blow

can't be a casualty of this life
can't stop until i end this strife

an uninhibited type of man
quite simply i am that i am
in but not of the world I see
striving to be the example
of whom to be

ix.
Man Plans God Laughs

...man plans GOD laughs

It is what it is
but not,
how it must be.

we are at
where we are;
& in time we will see.

if our fate
is written,
in stone or sand.

is this life
in our control?
or is it all out of our hands?

...GOD laughs,
in the face of man's careful plans.

X.
Who I Aim To Be

Who I aim to be
Is better than who I am
Seeking the lessons for growth
In all of life's situations

Choosing knowledge over ignorance
Humility over pride
Reality over fantasy
And love over hate

With my movements choreographed
Carefully predetermined
Yet agile and flexible
Built for any situation

As who I aim to be
Is better than who I am
Seeking the lessons for growth
In all of life's situations

It is with this clarity I maintain
A peaceful mind centred in logic

A truthful mouth void of scorn
And a pure heart to lead the way

The steady patience of a man
That rides a stubborn donkey
When dealing with those who lean
Heavily on their own misunderstanding

I possess a spirit unbreakable
I am an uncontained soul
With a shine that won't rust
A solid somebody you can trust

As who I aim to be
Is better than who I am
Seeking the lessons for growth
In all of life's situations

xi.
Because

...because rivers and tears flow
constant motion
never still

moving on
the only way
to release
all of the pain

...because afros and lilies grow
tall and high
towards the sun

shoulders back
heads to the sky
we walk proud
feeling high

...because I said
that I will
a promise made
only to you

with onlookers
looking on.

I am the man
who's earned your love
when we met
so long ago

at that time
I was committed
to which I've
never relented

nor wavered
or regretted
simply savoured
all of the moments

...because we are one
joined through a union
beyond the physical
a higher level
through our souls

...because I love you

xii.
How You Will Be Judged

words have so much meaning
deeds have even more
our conduct towards each other
is how we will be judged

be careful of your thoughts
as they translate to words
and influence your actions
tell all who you are

you say
"i was under stress"
this life game is so tough

or that
"i was inebriated"
the mind does need a break

these conditions that you speak of
are not odd or strange at all
you use them as an excuse
but the real you is revealed

words have so much meaning
deeds have even more
our conduct towards each other
is how we will be judged

xiii.
Care Giver

out of all
that i have given to you
it is your care
that i am most proud of

it started with a promise
to be your friend
and put you first
place your feelings
before my own

then there was my heart
it came with an engagement ring
followed by a gold band
i sealed the deal
and married you

you've always had all my support
for your wild adventures
and crazy ideas
conjured up
from your creative mind

i serve you now
at your request
giving you all that you need
moments that are pleasureful
a life that is unforgettable

out of all
that i have given to you
it is your care
that i am most proud of

xiv.
I use my words with action

i use my words
in a voice deep
grand and clear

full and loud
healing words
with actions that speak
even louder

for a love
that's endured
through the tests

over all this time
all these years
the good and bad

for a you and me
an us and we

that's closer
and grows
even stronger

could not have
imagined
from that day

fate filled day
love was claimed
in our naive teens

in my wildest
of dreams
till this day
we'd still be

inseparable
and happy together

so i tread on
with a faith
that's strong
yes the years
been long

though bear
the gift of strength
to carry on
with my mission

to use my words
in a voice deep
grand and clear

full and loud
healing words
with actions that speak
even louder

XV.
Into You

from first we met
i've been
into you
and wanted to get
into you

your spirit took me
and held me close
mesmerized
and captured me

the crowd they said
i was whipped by you
the P done got me
and worked its spell

they lacked the vision
they could not see
yet it was clear to me
my sights were far

your beauty drew me
your words soothed me
your body rocked me
your vibe stalked me

of pure soul
and strong mind
simply a visionary
into you was my future

from first we met
i've been
into you
and wanted to get
into you

xvi.
Keep Hearing You

at times it is your words
carefully selected
lacking quantity
not quality

a gem when you share
an inner look
into your being
into you

you are truly well
content
still
but still there

more times it is the clues
that you reveal
while trying to hide
the complex puzzle
that is you

a constant challenge
i find your pieces

the picture changes
i start anew

most times it is your smile
front gapped teeth perfection
deep dimples
bright hopeful eyes

my motivation
to keep persisting
for this reward
its worth the challenge

all times it is my purpose
to keep you healthy
keep you happy
keep listening

to keep hearing you

xvii.
Naive Teens

The sounds of our laughter that filled the air.
The movement of our bodies dancing through life, without a care.
The comfort of knowing, we are all we need.
All this created in the naivety of our teens.

The sounds of our cries working through the pain.
The movement of tears, down our eyes, as we search for blame.
The comfort of knowing, I got you and you got me.
All this created in the naivety of our teens.

The sound of contentment having passed through the storm.
The movement to the next phase, time moves on, this is the norm.
The comfort of the blessing of yet another day.
All this created in the naivety of our teens.

Life's lessons we've lived, grown, and stayed strong.
Fell down, stood up, brushed off and moved on.
The sounds, the movement and comforts derived.
From how we've lived, loved, laughed, and cried.

Not a believer in coincidence, chance, accidents or magical themes.
All this We truly created....
in the naivety of our teens.

xviii.
Naturally

Naturally
I would love you
And I have loved you
Naturally

From pig tails to perm
Puffs to jheri curl
From afro to weave
Braids to bob
Give me bantu knots and cornrows
As I love you most natural
Naturally

Whether done up or toned down
Hair and nails did or not
Four inch heals or sandals
Stripper boots or feet that are bare
I release you from all pretenses
As I love you most natural
Naturally

Face makeup or naked and uncovered
Waxed and lined or wild and free

Full brazilian or under cover
I am ready to be your explorer
As I love you most natural
Naturally

We have been all the things
That there are to be
I've seen all of you that there is to see
I do know you and you do know me
I make no demands of who you should be
Only that I love you most natural

Naturally
I would love you
And I have loved you
Naturally

xix.
Never Let You Go

i was not looking
i just turned your way
my eyes caught you
so i threw my line

you were captivating
so i captured you
and-drew you closer
never to let you go

from that day
i've never been alone
you've made my life
became my breath

so I bought some rings
breathing nervously
asked you to be my wife
the rest is OUR story

now decades with you
two children deep

you were paused
so my breath stopped

you continued on
my breathing restarted
now you're a different you
but still the same

me beyond thankful
my heart's elated
OUR time till OUR end
will never be wasted

i am now looking
always turned your way
catching you with my eyes
and throwing you my lines

you still captivating
i have captured you
draw you closer
will never let you go

XX.
Our Story

you have my heart
please hold it close to you
treat it with care
don't let it leave your view

the only one I have
so treat it properly
don't take it for granted
this precious property

it belongs to you
there is no mystery
from my eyes met yours
the rest is OUR story

you gave me your heart
a gift so special to me
it's mine to the end
a no return policy

these gifts we've shared
created a life of love

with two beautiful boys
a family ordained from above

till death does its part
on this earth we will be
OUR souls in lock step
the rest is OUR story

xxi.
Your Silence

Your silence is foreign
It was not who you were
You had so many words
Often creating some of your own

Your mind never stopped
Kept up a grueling pace
Never relenting never allowing
Your words to catch up

Your mind keeps running
But your words no longer follow
Instead opting out of the race
No longer tied to the demanding pace

So, you stand in your silence
But I still hear you loud and clear
Speaking in movements and expressions
And blessing me with scarce words

But how it is
Is not how it must be

So I work with you
To help you find the words

That will out pace your mind

Chapter 2

Broken On Arrival

i.
Broken

we are,
and have been,
from that day—
broken.

damaged,
fractured,
since illness crashed
our lives, our world.

a lifetime has passed
between what was,
and what is.
but possibilities breed hope.

of what could,
what should, and will be.
you are who you were
deep inside, the same to me.

the one i fell for,
and built a life with.

who holds my heart, my love
that I freely give.

life's trials and tribulations
near ends and new beginnings.
we've been through it, and
passed through the other side.

yes broken, but this story
is nowhere near its end.
there's more pages and chapters,
before this tale has been told.

ii.
Doomed

afterall.
aint we all just...
it's inescapable,
a by-product of life itself.
DOOMED.

it is our fate.
it is written,
it is to be & must
be.

here today,
gone tomorrow.
literally.

we have this time,
the time in between
& the freedom to spend it.

will you be selfless?
use your time,
in service of others.

will you be empathetic?
compassionate,
exuding love & understanding.

will you be wise?
not waste,
this precious gift

afterall.
aint we all just...
it's inescapable,
a by-product of life itself.
DOOMED.

iii.
Twisted

At times I am twisted
Bent out of shape
Turned all around
My upside will be down

At times I am inflexible
Tightly configured
Immovable from my position
Pained from manipulation

At times I am unaware
Blind to my options
Drained of all hope
With my tank on empty

And then the sun will rise
With its illuminating rays
Brightening my world
And enlightening me

And then the breeze will blow
Though visible only by touch

It breathes life around me
And also within me

Allowing me to become in tune
With all that surrounds me
Now able to move and flow
To counter life's twists and turns

Allowing me to become pliable
Eased and unwound
Freed from life's strains
Released from its pains

Now mindful and open
With my faith restored
Armed with the knowledge
The answers are within me

iv.
Gluttony

There is enough
For each one of us
None of us is greater
Than the other
Whether man or woman

It is access
That separates us
The privilege to have excess
To the detriment of another's success

It is a sin
that we all just
Accept the way that it is
And show disdain towards those who don't

Those damn have nots
They don't have enough
Because of something that they did
And our greed is just not relevant

It is their dreams
Their lacking desires

If they only dreamt of bright bootstraps
And pulled on them for themselves

But it is our sin
That we can sit and watch
The suffering and poverty
As we fill our mouths and sip our tea

There is enough
For each one of us
None of us is greater
Than the other
Whether man or woman

V.
Contradiction

How do you act
When no one is watching
Is it the same
As when we all see you

They say we should dance
Like there are no eyes upon us
Yet act in a way
As if everyone is watching

What is done in the dark
Comes out in plain sight
Reconcile who you are
Contradictions cause shame in the light

vi.
I am Open

And I am.
I have been and remain
Open.
In hopes that you will also be.

I was.
At first arrival a blank slate.
A shiny front and back cover
With pages yet to be filled.

Time has passed
The pages are filling up.
And I am, still here
Yet changed.

Yes changed.
Developed.
Into an overwhelming and overwhelmed,
Confident and insecure
well put together chaotic mess.

And I am.
I have been and remain

Open.
In hopes that you will also be.

With the covers now worn and
completed pages revealed.
It is my duty to share this journey
With you.

So my life I share
For you to hear.
As I have something to teach,
For you to learn.

As my journey,
Its flaws and imperfections
Are the norm and to be embraced.
Its learnings are to be treasured and passed on.

And I am.
I have been and remain
Open.
In hopes that you will also be.

vii.
Look Much Deeper

Look much deeper
Beyond the surface
Further than
Your eyes can see

That's the place
Where I will be
A hidden secret
And grand mystery

Use all of your senses
To guide your way
And navigate
This big reveal

What you'll find
Will be extraordinary
Unexpected
And unforeseen

A shocking surprise
You may love or despise

But no longer unknown
Once found and exposed

My joy from LOVE
That's been nurtured in my life
Tears from pain
That had crushed my soul

The flame of anger
Heated by my disappointments
The cool of my calmness
Healed and soothed by time

My bumpy rollercoaster
With deep slopes and tight turns
And more times than not
Moving upside down

My evil fun house
With trick mirrors and shifty floors
Keeping me terrified and amused
But mostly searching for more

Stay focused and resilient
Keep on with your search
You'll find both faith and hope
The secret of how I cope

Look much deeper
Beyond the surface
Further than
Your eyes can see

viii.
More Than The Sum

More than your eyes
So open and bright
That offer a small glimpse
Into your beautiful soul

More than your smile
That shines like a beacon
Inspite of the conditions
Whether rain or shine

More than your frame
Barely five feet tall
That attracted me
At first from behind

More than your beauty
Of which I remain lost
Within and around
You're the only queen I crown

More than your mind
That motivates and inspires
Greatness and accountability

In all
In me

More than a survivor
More than what life has stolen
More than what it has cost
More than all that was lost

This life is not a simple equation
It is never defined by the losses
You are more than
More than the sum of it all

ix.
My Tears

Water.
Seen by you through my sweat and my tears. An expression of my joys, stresses and fears.

Part of me, sixty percent of my makeup.
Revealed through life's circumstances by simply showing up.

When I am heated with rage to cool my anger.
When I am overcome with happiness to express my joy.
When I run through my memories in times of reflection. As I lock in and hold on to precious moments of the past.

Water.
Seen by you through my sweat and my tears. An expression of my joys, stresses and fears.

Necessary for me to get through life's ebbs and flows.
The process to cleanse, purge and purify my soul.
Lets me feel what is needed then to let it all go.

They say that a man ain't supposed to cry. Be a vessel with no feelings with eyes bone dry.

Just ignore all the pain and shift all the blame. Be a real man and be driven insane.

No longer do I worry about what they say.
Now open to emotions especially my pain.
No shame in my game or stutter in my step.
I now own my feelings and take pride that I've wept.

Water.
Seen by you through my sweat and my tears. An expression of my joys, stresses and fears.

X.
Pre-Judge-Us

a false narrative
a controversy

one in which the subject
did not create or promote
and surely does not own

it precedes its subjects
beating them to every room
just before they enter

just prior to
in the nick of time

in the shadows
is where its working

the elephant in the room
it lingers and hovers
overpowers reality

an unwelcomed guest
a squatter
intent on staying

driven by hate
guided by fear
with the sole purpose
to survive

Ironically sharing
the purpose
of its subjects
to survive

Fulfilling its purpose
to their detriment

truly successful
when they believe
the false narrative

a bottomless pit
for this bottom dweller

always hungry
never satisfied

creating a void
ignorance prevailing

yet its life is fragile
not in its control

depending on us
for its existence

sadly, WE have been
a dependable friend

xi.
My Pride

please bear with me
& stand by my side
it will take some time
to manage my pride

not derived from pleasure
from joy
comfort or satisfaction

not resulting from beauty
& LOVE shared
through our interaction

please bear with me
& stand by my side
it will take some time
to manage my pride

as ego and pain
came along for this ride

& fear and shame
traveled right by their side

please bear with me
& stand by my side
it will take some time
to manage my pride

now filled with illusions
delusions
confusions of grandeur

the subconscious goal
to hide not reveal
conceal the hurt & the anger

this time now
my coming of age
i'm ready & willing
to turn the page

the production is over
this play won't resume
it has come to a hault
has reached it's end

gone are the costumes
the script and the masks
& with these things
the need to pretend

question my resolve
but not my intent
for I am human & flawed
striving to be heaven sent

please bear with me
& stand by my side
it will take some time
to manage my pride

xii.
Stroke!

...then deceived.
by a crook; a thief
who travelled alone,
by day or was it night.
from far or maybe near.

who knocked you down;
paralyzed you.
left you speechless
& terrorized you.

robbed your mind,
& stole your moves.
took your memories,
& left you stranded.

life & its promises,
they're always empty.
only a comfort,
to those who are fools.

not constrained by feelings,
or moved by emotions.

no sense of justice,
having no wrongs to right.

...now restored yet humbled;
by the fragility of life.
your palette was emptied
you rush to fill the space.

rebuilding your life,
with no time to waste.
realigning priorities,
putting the pieces in place.

retracing your steps,
though faded & worn.
who you will become,
not the you that was;
but the you reborn.

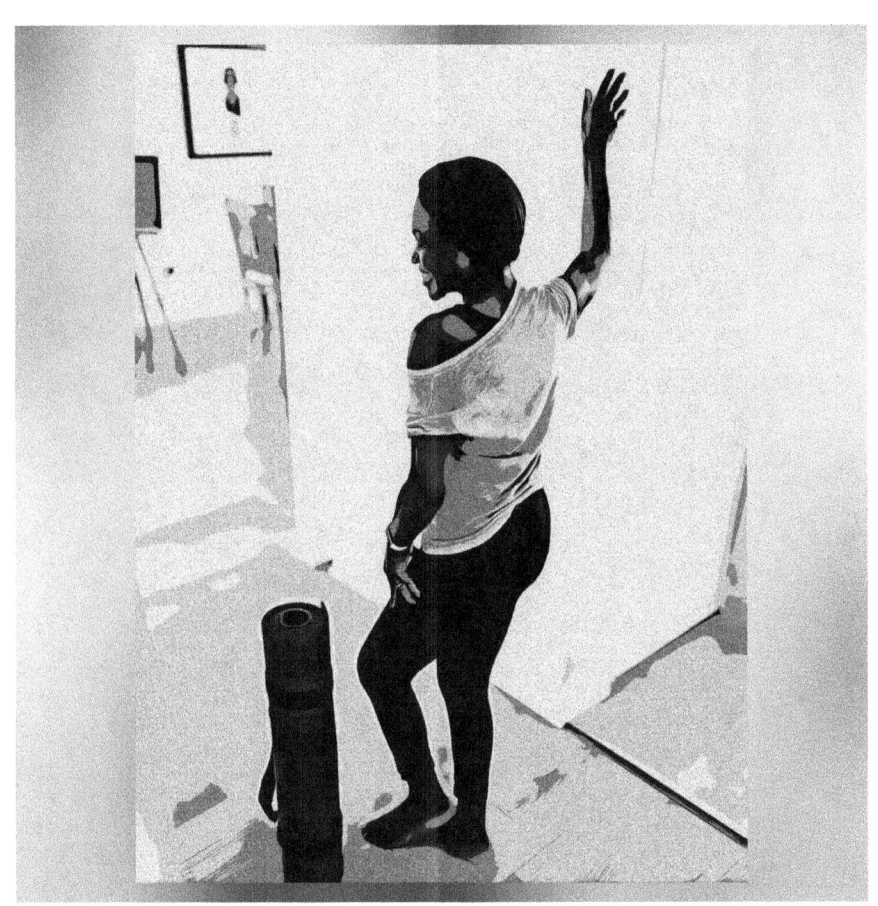

Chapter 3

The Quest

i.
Do Right

to seek and find
the answers to questions
to try to do
the best for the situation

to learn past lessons
and change our present
to right the wrongs
and live in redemption

to keep the search going
and sustain a safe pace
to be steadfast for the journey
and maintain resilience

to take care with the steps
and watch their placement
to hold patience as a virtue
and be the example

to be the light
in the midst of the storm
to lead first with love
and be open to the blessings

ii.
Our Quest

The journey is unknown, unchartered and awaiting exploration.

There are many stops on the path, each offering an experience, an opportunity or lesson of some sort.

Yet to be deciphered, yet to reveal the answers we seek.

Though we are in this together, our journey's are taken individually and the paths are isolated.

We each must make our own way.
It is a journey of a lifetime, that will take a lifetime to complete.

What we receive out of it, depends on the paths taken.

The answers we get...
Will have to wait till the end, of our quest.

iii.
…in search of

Lost, to be found.
Missing right in front of me.
Clouded, in the clear brightness of the day.

You.
Who I am in search of.

A beautiful struggle.
With many promises, few comforts
And rewards sparsely scattered on the way.

All for you.
Who I am in search of.

It requires much of me,
Because in searching for you
I have found me.
What I am made of and what makes me, me.

Is you.
Who I am in search of.

It is what I always knew
And never spoke of.
You are the key to me,
Unlocking the best man that I can be.

You.
Who I am in search of.

So, I plan my steps
And document my journey.
Broadcasting my travels throughout the four corners of this earth.
Letting everyone know.

It is you.
Who I am in search of.

In hopes of attracting those who've travelled before.
Those who share my journey.
Those who unknowingly hold a clue, answer, or solution.
Those who can help me solve the puzzle that is.

You.
Who I am in search of.

iv.
Moments

the feelings will last
the memory will fade
be wise with your time
take care of each moment

leaving you more than
adding to you
my only goal
with each interaction

moving through time
traveling within
navigating between
the moments with purpose

uncertainty looms
the distance & time
the great unknown
the length of our journey

the road will run out
our time will end

leaving the legacy
of all of the moments

making the most of
making them pleasant
making them count
keeping love in the moments

the feelings will last
the memory will fade
be wise with your time
take care of each moment

V.
i and i survive

through the harsh terrain
bitter cold winds
into the night i go
the stars my only light

i and i survive

off of the grid
no gps or street signs
no tour guide
no compass or map

i and i survive

facing all my fears
crying all my tears
processing all my emotions
building my mind body and soul

i and i survive

with food as my medicine
my body now my temple

sharpening my mind
and nourishing my soul

i and i survive

the slings and arrows
spears and bullets
and weapons of mass seduction
waged in our self destruction

i and i survive

no longer distracted
now moving with focus
tunnel vision
making my time count

counting each day
counting the days
understanding my ways
making my way through time

as time will take my body
this temporary vessel
yet my soul and my spirit
beliefs and ideas will remain

this is my victory as
i and i survive

vi.
Dinner with Old Friends

We are connected.
Bonded, joined together.
Founded on joint experiences.
Events that have long past.

Memories degrade, fade.
Accounts of events differ, change.
There is no frustration though.
The good vibes of our time, remain.

Catching up on the time since.
Marriage, children, and grands.
Divorce, restarts and plans.
Friends, with and without benefits.

Sharing our triumphs and victories.
Sicknesses, and near ends.
Our loves, and our losses.
This life comes at a great cost.

Memories degrade, fade.
Accounts of events differ, change.
There is no frustration though.
The good vibes of our time, remain.

vii.
Give it back to you

It feels good to receive
and even better to give
With the gift of your LOVE
I'll give you back so much more

Be wise of when
You choose to gift it
As you may have unknowingly
Bit off more than you can chew

I'll receive your LOVE gracefully
And return it ten fold
So, when I give back
You'll need to hold on

Hold on to your breath
And something secure
'Cause what you'll receive
Will surely blow your mind

I will take you to school
Where you'll learn from my class
The lessons built out of

My life
My past

I'll take my time
Start you out real slow
Build anticipation
Of my LOVE as it grows

We'll witness it together
As it reaches its height
Right before it explodes
And bonds us for life

It feels good to receive
and even better to give
With the gift of your LOVE
I'll give you back so much more

viii.
Goodbye Hello

You see I traveled so far
To say goodbye
But you are so far
From gone

I sung you a song
Only my voice as the band
"A long time gal me nevah see you
Come mek me hold your hand"

Your hand raised up
And tightly held mine
Your eyes locked on
Displaying strong life signs

At first appearance
You're missing and lost
With movements limited
Showing Illnesses cost

But your strength shines through
With resilience and defiance

Although no words as yet form
Cutting through your silence

I see It's not your time
There's more from you to get
More to learn from you to share
Before your sun will finally set

You see I traveled so far
To say goodbye
But you are so far
From gone

ix.
It's in the Air

There is a change
In the air

A newness a rebirth
In the air

Renewing my spirit
And guiding my soul
To explore this new feeling
In the air

There is an awakening
In the air

Endless possibilities
In the air

To explore and discover
Without pause or doubt
There is fearlessness
In the air

I will be naked and exposed
In the air

With no cover or protection
In the air

I'll Ignore the risk of failure
And take my chances
To experience
The LOVE rebirth and growth
In the air

X.
My Mantra

to seek and find
the answers to questions
to try to do
the best for the situation

to learn past lessons
and change the present
to right past wrongs
and live in redemption

to keep the search going
and sustain a safe pace
to be steadfast for the journey
and maintain resilience

to take care with the steps
and watch their placement
to hold patience as a virtue
and be the example

to be the light
in the midst of the storm
to lead first with love
and be open to blessings

xi.
Me, Myself, and I

met up with some friends today
who i've known from...
i can remember

no real purpose in the meeting
just touchin' base
restoring our connections

we do this from time to time
but never often enough
life gets in the way most times

we loose track of ourselves
never making the time
to stop reflect and connect

my first friend; name is me
he was struggling
with the cards
he has been dealt

i offered sympathetic ears
comfort

truly knowing
how he felt

my other friend; name is myself
he was exhausted
wearing too many hats

i reminded him
of the one head he has
and only one at a time
a hat can fit

as for i; my story has been written
i even shout it out loud
my way of processing feelings
rather than bury them
in a linen shroud

we laughed cried and rejoiced
truly enjoyed our time
sadly life came calling once again
signalling our time to depart

there were promises
to meet real soon
not letting too much time pass
we said our goodbyes till next time
till then these good vibes must last

from when i...
met up with some friends
who i've known from...
i can remember

xii.
That Place

a quest to find
a peaceful space
where my mind can be
clear and free

a lifetime journey
to regain then reclaim
and at its end
maintain
my sanity
my humanity

in search of that place
where i can be
true to me
truly me

where i am
unmonitored and unrestricted
freed from the expectations
released from the limitations

where i am open
to the possibilities
open to fail and free fall
open to stand and grow tall

this is that place
where i can be
true to me
truly me

at times i feel
stuck and out of place
ignored and displaced
alone and misplaced

in this time
i will withdraw
mute the crowd
and shut off its noise

now amplified
are my thoughts and my intensions
laser focused
on my purpose

this is my space
i found that place
where i can be
true to me
truly me

xiii.
The Drum

To the land of the drum
Where we descend from
From those who came from before

To where Jah-make-ya (Jamaica)
Our parents birthplace
The land of the drum and the bass

With rhythms that soothe
Guide and move
And change moods with a simple groove

The power of the beat
That hits so sweet
And takes all the pain away

It is my will
For it to be as it was
And to make our time stand still

As we dance
I'll hold your hand

And you'll hold mine
We will be transported back in time

To the land of the drum
Where we descend from
From those who came from before

To where Jah-make-ya (Jamaica)
Our parents birthplace
The land of the drum and the bass

Chapter 4

Finding
Redemption

i.
First Things First

...but first i live.
leaning in on love
followed closely,
by forgiveness.

of my self,
then of those around me.
my errors human,
as are those belonging to you.

requesting of you,
nothing more,
nothing less,
than i demand of me.

walking with you,
a mile in your shoes.
standing, running, and dancing
in your feet.

learning from you,
through our interactions.

knowing who you are,
teaches me who i am.

there is untapped potential,
and multiple possibilities,
of what could be—
in my quest to be the best me.

...but first i live.
leaning in on love
followed closely,
by forgiveness.

of my self,
then of those around me.
my errors human,
as are those belonging to you.

ii.
It's Not Me, It's You

Your definition of me depends on your definition of you.
Where I fit depends on what you are missing.

I can be a friend to depend on, or a foe never to cross.
A bad habit to lose, or a trusted confidant to hold.
A hero just a call away, or a nemesis to magnify your problems.

Your definition of me depends on your definition of you.
Where I fit depends on what you are missing.

Perspectives can be clouded by feelings and facts often get in the way.
My role is not to play second fiddle to your emotions,
But to be an inconvenient truth.

Your definition of me depends on your definition of you.
Where I fit depends on what you are missing.

Look beyond.
Your mask, your costume, and false pretenses.
Now exposed and transparent, the journey to self can begin.

Your definition of me depends on your definition of you.
Where I fit depends on what you are missing.

After all, It's not me.
It's you.

iii.
To Where Our Souls Reside

to have
and to hold
i needed to possess you
grasp and caress you
love and undress you

from this day forward
i meant it
forever
beyond our time on this rock
to where our souls will reside

for better
for worse
it's not always been easy
but we travel the path
where goodness and mercy must follow

for richer
for poorer
our cup runneth over

we have more than our needs
a life filled with love

in sickness
and in health
my devotion's unwavering
it's been tested by time
i ain't tapping out

to love
and to cherish
is this even a question
i care for you dearly
and my love making is legendary

until death
do us part
it is what i promised
what i signed up for

it's just a transition

we will see about this one
this one troubles me
you are me and I am you
there is no me without you

i meant it
forever
beyond our time on this rock
to where our souls will reside

iv.
Already Ready

the realization
we will not be
as we once were
and perhaps should never be
after all
it's been done...

already

the first time around
the teachings were learned
now stored and backed up
we are grown and...

ready

for all these years
to have passed
to only trace past steps
would only reveal
that we are not...

ready

in a state of change
constant evolution
aware and agile
finally proving to each other
that for this life
we are definitely

already...
ready

V.

Face to Face

There is no choice.
We must deal with it.
We are encompassed.
No where to hide or run.

As we walk side by side,
Through it.
We are face to face,
With it.

Fear. It is...
Ever present.
A trusted friend,
And constant foe.

A reminder of boundaries.
Limitations.
The walls we build.
We must—we will—breakthrough.

For now we work, continuously.
In the shadows.

Behind the scenes and
Out of the spotlight.

Improving through consistency,
Rewarded by results.
Prayer through action,
Glory going to the Most High.

There is no choice.
We must deal with it.
We are encompassed.
No where to hide or run.

As we walk side by side,
Through it.
We are face to face,
With it.

vi.
Life Force

It is that powerful energy
Resonating vibrations
Of good feelings
That is essential to my life force

I watch my levels closely
In case they get too low
And avoid situations
That drain or corrupt it

As when the intention is to sap and steal
My energy
My time
It is wise not to be sucked into this vortex

Vibrations feed my soul
Protect me and calm me
Guide and uplift me
The key to how I make it through each day

Providing hope
For a future

And the strength
To make this future come true

It is that powerful energy
Resonating vibrations
Of good feelings
That is essential to my life force

vii.
My Promise to You

i promise

to disappoint you
and fall short of your expectations
to not live up to
the who you perceive me to be

to let you down
at times rather harshly
to turn my back on your emotions
and in that moment be free of guilt

to have my frustrations
get the better of me
and be present and accounted for
transparent for you to see

to let anger win some battles
and wallow in self pity
and spend precious time
drowning in my own tears

and i promise

to stop and reflect
analyze and assess
my actions and how they
have impacted you

to always be with you
not leave you down
pick you up from the hurt
even when i am the cause

to never stop trying
and shoot for the stars
despite the countless times
my aim has come short

and finally, I promise

to have love win over hate
and be ruled by my heart
be sound in my thoughts
and kind with my words

this is my promise to you

viii.
My Song

this is my song
the story that i've lived

only these lyrics
you will hear
no background music
yet to share

this is my song
the story that i've lived

with sound
rhythm and rhymes
heart beats and syncopation

to realign my mind
my soul
my spirit
with my situation

this is my song
the story that i've lived

it is all the things
that i have been
from all the places
that i have seen

a love story and tragedy
a great loss and victory
listen to it to set the mood

to make love
to fight your demons
to cause a disturbance
to meditate when you
need to be soothed

this is my song
the story that i've lived

an isolated extrovert
suffering from a jolly depression
who can be soft or hard
when he loves and hates

yet filled with hope
that to the end
there are lessons in this
a purpose a meaning
to my current state

this is my song
the story that i've lived

ix.
My Time

as long as i am
it is my time

as long as i feel
the day's warmth
under the sun's shine
the night's coolness
under the moon's light

as long as i reside
on this rock
travelling through space
spinning and tilting
turning around
bending around
the sun

as long as i am
it is my time

for i am still here
breathing the air

taking up space
and spending my days

living and learning
loving and serving
yearning and burning
for better days
and simpler ways

...of being

i remain hopeful though
as in me it rings
internal
eternal

hope
for it i will work forever
infinitely
without regard for time

for
as long as i am
it will be
my time

X.
My Voice

it is my choice
this
how i use my voice

existing in the here & now
choosing not to spend time
in the past & the future

remaining here
in a vibrant external world
restricting internal back talk
between me
myself
& i

it is my choice
this
how i use my voice

staying positive
with focus & concentration
releasing all that is negative

committed to learn & grow
without the cost of another's
ignorance & stagnation

it is my choice
this
how i use my voice

loving unconditionally
unconflicted
regardless of actions
that should cause conflict

living by codes & principles
in a world
lacking of these ancient practices

it is my choice
this
how i use my voice

choosing happiness
an act of defiance
despite evidence to the contrary

living a life of LOVE & hope
in a world filled with
conflict & despair

it is my choice
this
how i use my voice

xi.
My Word

my offer, a simple one.
to back the words i speak
purposely,
consistently, with action.

this is my currency;
what i truly own
in this life
can't be taken away from me.

my word,
my bond,
our connection: me to you
and you to me.

no dependencies,
not hedged on convenience.
no backtracking,
not based on fair-weather.

here for you
offering protection,

to work with you
providing steady direction.

a foundation, a base,
that you can rely on.
a pillar in your life,
you can surely depend on.

my offer, a simple one.
to back the words i speak
purposely,
consistently, with action.

xii.
Naked

What motivates you
From day-to-day

And gives you power
To find your way

Propels and moves you
To a sustainable pace

The fuel you'll need
To endure life's race

Is it love
Is it hate
That will fill up your tank

Is it empathy
Is it greed
The currency you will bank

Your decisions are key
Each a critical choice

What you choose to embrace
Speaks louder than your voice

You may conceal and hide
Your truths and desires

Change the wolf to a lamb
Pour water on your fire

But this life is a marathon
And deception is a sprint

Authenticity is easier
Although counter to what you think

This lesson is an old one
But make your call

This life will expose you
Like the bare tree in the fall

xiii.
Not As They Seem

there are levels to this
things are not as they seem

the surface may be
shiny and new
and emanate beauty
it is the layers that reveal
the true and ugly view

first sight may be unpleasant
but go deeper a little further
you could reveal with a closer look
the beauty you initially mistook

there are levels to this
things are not as they seem

the book can't be told
by simply skimming the cover
you can't be known in an instant
by being watched from a distance

take the time and make the space
be wary of people
and their associations
put yourself first always
be your number one consideration

your integrity
and wise reflection
from ill conceived motivations
this is and will be
your key protection

there are levels to this
things are not as they seem

xiv.
Pains Purpose

pain is essential
integral to our existence
the physical experience
we call life

it is our confidante
warning and protecting
yielding and preventing
harm from continuing

it is our nemesis
scolding and rebuking
inflicting and punishing
when snubbed or ignored

an unwelcomed guest
uninvited
crashing your world
changing your vibe

a thief in the night
catching you off guard

stealing from you
leaving you less than

there is purpose
a lesson to learn
a message to relay
and a price to pay

pain will bend you
take care not to break
as after
it mends you and
healing begins

XV.
Perfect

And you are just perfect. Just perfect for me.

You move through this life in barely a five-foot frame, with a crown of twists atop your head.
Petite in size yet grand in so many ways: personality, ambition, dreams, and love.

And you are just perfect. Just perfect for me.

Beautiful. Your deep chocolate skin blessed by the sun, passed on from those who came from before.
You: a shining example of your tropical home, the culture, food, music, and all the traditions.

And you are just perfect. Just perfect for me.

Large, bright, and brown are your eyes, the windows to the journey of your wondering soul.
A cute flat nose and dimpled gap teeth smile, a welcoming to your world filled with love.

And you are just perfect. Just perfect for me.

But have I told you this enough?
It's always the right time to.
Time is never wrong.

Are you open to hear it?
Can you still hear me, and will you remember?

I don't care if you can't, I will not stop saying...
I love you.

And you are just perfect. Just perfect for me.

xvi.
Purpose

our quest
searching for the why
the reasons
we exist in the here
& now

our path
the road we travel
learning life's lessons
no free rides
there is a price to pay

our journey
at first roaming aimlessly
unguided
standing for nothing
falling for everything

our movements
provide perspective
direction & focus

as we find the clues
unlocking the reasons why

once found
there is breath
there is life
there is love
...there is purpose

xvii.
The Notes Not Played

Watch with your third eye
To read in-between the lines
It is the notes that are not played
That distinguishes the music that we hear

I receive what is communicated
But look at all that comes with it
Watching the things that are not done
Listening to the words that are not spoken

I never simply just rely on
Or put all of my dependence on
My ears filled up with wax
Or my eyes that sometimes lie

It is the choices that are made
That display the deceit that is staged
But amongst the actions that are rejected
Tells the truth and reveals intention

Be on the look out for the liar
And their trusted companion snitch

They travel together day and night
But snitch confesses in the brightness of the light

See all of the words that are written
Listen to all the notes that are played
As they provide us with a record
Of what has occurred and what's being portrayed

I will urge you time and time again
Before each day comes to an end
To study those who you call foe
And those who you define as a friend

Watch with your third eye
To read in-between the lines
It is the notes that are not played
That distinguishes the music that we hear

xviii.
The Patient Patient

With fulfillment delayed
Comes the lesson of patience
Unable to control the duration
The time

Life's fragile state
Changed in an instant
Now in search
Of a life that once was

Once a patient now patient
Recovery takes patience
Time not the enemy
And not always your friend

The clock is ticking
Its noise deafening
Its movement an illusion
Of our perception

Cherish the moments
The triumphs
The memories

The journey is long
And it has just begun

xix.
The Process

Trusting in the process
But constantly looking ahead of it
Anticipating the end
Yet benefiting from the foreplay

As racing to the finish
Anxious and impatient
Will reduce the results
And the rush on arrival

Taking several steps forward
And sometimes as many backwards
Helps improve the final goal
And will propel you much further

Trusting in the process
But constantly looking ahead of it
Anticipating the end
Yet benefiting from the foreplay

XX.
Weapon

Victor or victim
Powerful or destitute
Master or the baited
What will you choose?

Prosecutor or persecuted
Doer or done to
Pimp or prostitute
Who will you be?

Happy or blue
Real or fake
Knowledgeable or ignorant
Is it so hard to decide?

Hater or hated
Armed or defenseless
To be or not to
Did you not think this out?

Sympathy or apathy
Honesty or deceit

Transparent or opaque
Do you think I can't see?

It is all within you
You can power your fate
With fate's weapons be careful
As they can also harm you

xxi.
Those Who Know Know

those who know
know

know the time before
won't let bygones be
bygones

see the change since
but not the changes
I've seen

since the time
since that day

those who know
know

know the struggle
feel my pain
catch my tears

know compassion
feel sympathy
offer empathy

giving too much
at times

pity
not required
its not that kind of party

those who know
know

your dignity non-negotiable
our love unconditional
never-ending

those who know
know

my devotion unrelenting
as is my tenderness
and my humanity

those who know
know

you
have always been
my option

and our life
worth the struggle

those who know
know

if you don't know
now you know...

xxii.
U Do U and I'll Do Me

Please...
U do U
& I'll do ME

Ain't that the way
It's supposed 2 B
Whether U agree
With who I B

Or if I'm down
With the U I C

Different voices
& their melodies
Create such beautiful
harmonies

So please...
U do U
& I'll do ME

Don't destroy
What could B

By hiding the U
Within the ME U C

Or if I conceal
The truth that is ME

We will not reach
Our destiny
Reducing options
Of what could B

So please …
U do U
& I'll do ME

At times WE will
break this rule
U know I like
2 act the fool

In those moments
WE let it out
B the freak
Scream & shout

Quite often it
takes a toll
If WE feel stuck
In OUR roles

There is but 1
Solution then

This is OUR moment
That is when...

I do U
& U do ME...
Please ;-)

xxiii.
The Stakes Is High

The stakes is high
And they have been since
With risks that cost life
And rewards that cheat death

The pain we bear today
Will bring joy in the future
Consistency is the key
Opening opportunities for tomorrow

Never wavering
Bending or buckling
A solid pillar and constant
Staying the course

A consistent leader
First through me
The ultimate example
Of who I am

I am energy
Electricity

A quiet storm
The calm and the force

On occasion my kindness
Has been mistaken
Erroneously defined
My humility for weakness

But I remain
Calm and undisturbed
Unchanged but aware of
That which is put upon me

These are the lessons
Life's mess life's shit
The thorns that cut deep
The blood let in our own making

The stakes is high
And they have been since
With risks that cost life
And rewards that cheat death

Epilogue

If it was just...
To hold you and caress you
To bathe you, dress and undress you
Each day
Then I would know

If it was just...
To oil your body and twist your hair
To look into your deep brown eyes
Have my deeds speak of my care
Then I would know

If it was just. . .
To update and prepare you
To nourish and nurture you
To let patience be my virtue
Then I would know

If it was just...
To move and motivate you
To Be with and masterly-debate you
To Be a cunning-linguist to you
Then I would know

If it was just...
To feed you and to f— you
To put you first above all priorities
To see your smile and hear your giggle
Then I would know

What I have learned is
ENOUGH

What I am doing is
ENOUGH

My love is
ENOUGH

That I am
ENOUGH

Acknowledgements

To those of you who have loved me, coddled me, raised my spirits, or simply been there for me. For those who have criticized me, held me accountable, and grounded me when I needed to be reminded of who I am and, most importantly, who I aim to be.

To you because you have all guided me and brought me closer towards the best version of me. Joined me willingly and at times unwillingly in my journey on this rock through the many cycles of triumphs, breakdowns, and rebuilding. We have shared this life in motion, in movement through time. And now the search for redemption, this journey of a lifetime. A journey not for the weak at heart or those with fair-weather intent.

As we stride forward together, I thank you for your commitment and endurance.

www.ingramcontent.com/pod-product-compliance
Lightning Source LLC
Chambersburg PA
CBHW071356120626
46546CB00002B/722